DISCOVER
The Aztec

by Barbara Brannon

Table of Contents

Introduction	2
Chapter 1 Where Did the Aztec Live?	4
Chapter 2 What Was Aztec Life Like?	8
Chapter 3 Why Were the Aztec Important?	12
Conclusion	18
Concept Map	20
Glossary	22
Index	24

Introduction

The **Aztec** lived long ago. The Aztec had a great **civilization**.

Words to Know

 Aztec

 calendar

 civilization

 Mexico

 North America

 pyramids

See the Glossary on page 22.

Chapter 1

Where Did the Aztec Live?

The Aztec lived in **North America**.
The Aztec lived in **Mexico**.

▲ Mexico is in North America.

The Aztec lived in cities.

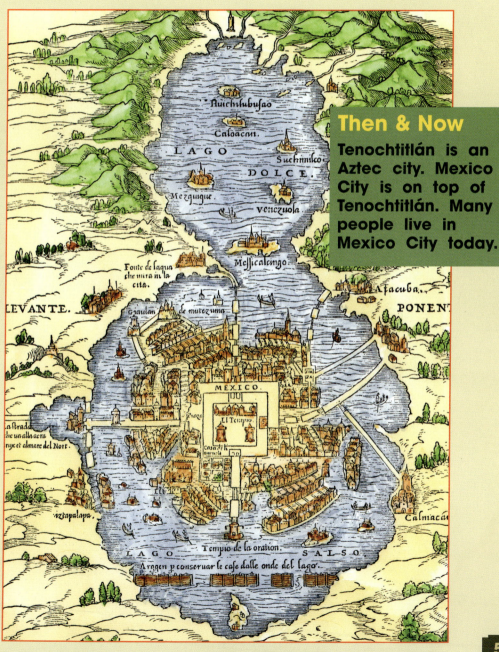

Then & Now
Tenochtitlán is an Aztec city. Mexico City is on top of Tenochtitlán. Many people live in Mexico City today.

▲ The Aztec had cities.

Chapter 1

The Aztec lived in villages.

▲ The Aztec had villages.

Where Did the Aztec Live?

The Aztec lived in homes.

▲ The Aztec had homes.

Chapter 2

What Was Aztec Life Like?

The Aztec had gardens.

Did You Know?
You can visit the gardens today.

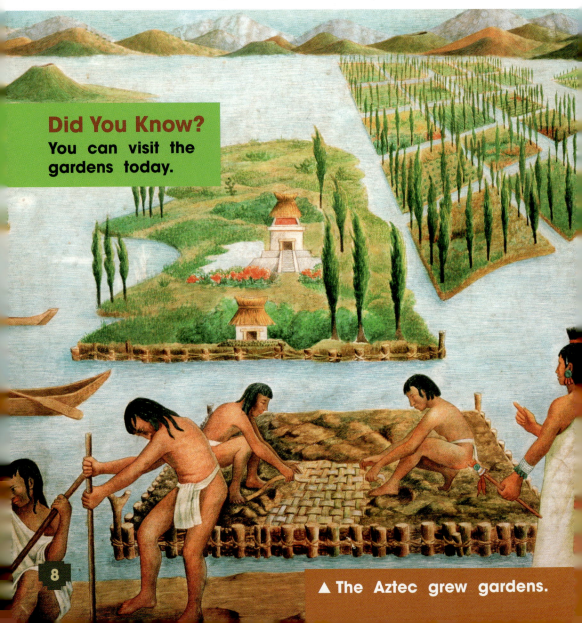

▲ The Aztec grew gardens.

The Aztec had farms. The Aztec had crops.

▲ The Aztec grew crops.

Chapter 2

The Aztec had markets.

▲ The Aztec went to markets.

What Was Aztec Life Like?

The Aztec had kings. The Aztec had temples.

The Aztec kings were important. ▶

▲ The Aztec went to temples.

Chapter 3

Why Were the Aztec Important?

The Aztec made a **calendar**.

▲ The Aztec had a calendar.

The Aztec made pottery.

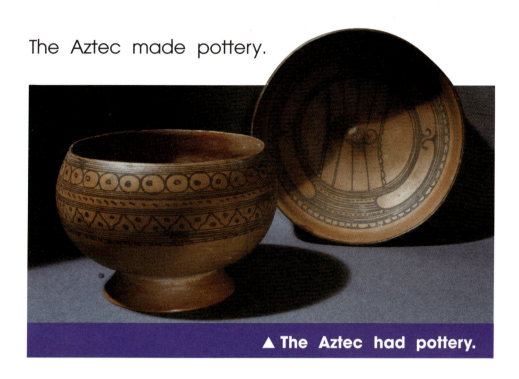

▲ The Aztec had pottery.

The Aztec made carvings.

▲ The Aztec had carvings.

Chapter 3

The Aztec made bridges.

▲ The Aztec had bridges.

The Aztec made aqueducts.

▲ The Aztec had aqueducts.

Why Were the Aztec Important?

The Aztec made terraces.

▲ The Aztec had terraces.

The Aztec made canals.

▲ The Aztec had canals.

15

Chapter 3

The Aztec made **pyramids**.

It's a Fact
This is the Pyramid of the Sun. People can still climb the pyramid.

▲ The Aztec had pyramids.

Why Were the Aztec Important?

The Aztec made tools.

▲ The Aztec had tools.

17

Conclusion

The Aztec had a great civilization.

Concept Map

The Aztec

Where Did the Aztec Live?

- North America
- Mexico
- cities
- villages
- homes

Glossary

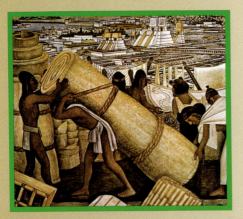

Aztec an ancient group of people

The **Aztec** made canals.

calendar a table showing the measurement of time

The Aztec made a **calendar**.

civilization a group of people who share ideas about living together

The Aztec had a great **civilization**.

Mexico land in North America

The Aztec lived in **Mexico**.

North America a continent

*The Aztec lived in **North America**.*

pyramids Aztec buildings

*The Aztec made **pyramids**.*

Index

aqueducts, 14, 21
Aztec, 2, 4–18, 20–21
bridges, 14, 21
calendar, 12, 21
canals, 15, 21
carvings, 13, 21
civilization, 2, 18
crops, 9, 21
farms, 9, 21
gardens, 8, 21
kings, 11, 21
markets, 10, 21
Mexico, 4, 20
North America, 4, 20
pottery, 13, 21
pyramids, 16, 21
temples, 11, 21